STOICISM

A Comprehensive Guide
To Stoicism and Stoic Philosophy

John Ferguson

Table of Contents

Introduction 1

Chapter One: Stoicism And Why You Should Be Interested 4

Chapter Two: The Origins Of Stoicism 11

Chapter Three: Stoic Philosophy And Virtues 18

Chapter Four: Eight Vital Stoic Principles To Live By 30

Chapter Five: Famous Stoics And How They Lived 40

Chapter Six: Stoicism In Modern Times 51

Chapter Seven: How Stoicism Can Help You 57

Chapter Eight: Twenty Stoic Exercises To Explore 63

Chapter Nine: Transform Your Life With These Five Stoic Techniques 70

Chapter Ten: Famous Stoic Quotes You Can Use Today 74

Conclusion 77

Introduction

Life is full of ups and downs. There are occurrences that catch us completely off-guard and leave us in a state of absolute shock. It could be one traumatic experience after the other and, most times, situations like these get in the way of our attaining genuine happiness. I mean, can you be truly happy when you heard that rumor about your workplace doing layoffs? Or maybe you just got that scary test result from your doctor. Whatever the case is, the fact remains that unfortunate events happen and when they do, the majority of us become distraught and extremely upset. While it is completely understandable to feel this way, Stoicism helps you discover how to deal with events like these when they do happen so that they do not affect your emotions and your happiness. Everyone wants to be happy. We all enjoy that sweet feeling that many people consider to be the main purpose of life but, sometimes, happiness can seem like an abstract idea that isn't really attainable. Is it possible to be genuinely happy? The answer is "Yes." Stoicism maintains that you can feel true happiness even in the midst of crises and unforeseen negative circumstances.

Stoicism started as far back as the 3rd Century BCE when Zeno of Citium would sit on a porch in Athens and share his theory with all who cared to listen. Over time, more people started to realize just how valuable this school of thought could be, and it started spreading across the Greek and Roman civilizations. People from various walks of life started to adopt Zeno of Citium's theories: from soldiers to playwrights, slaves to emperors, these theories most definitely hold untapped treasures many of us are not so familiar with. If you opened this guide, you're likely wondering what Stoicism is about and if it can actually be practiced in this era as well. Maybe you've wondered who present-day Stoics really are and how this approach to life benefits them, especially in the modern times we live in. How is a school of thought that was created hundreds of years ago still relevant and beneficial to its practitioners in the 21st Century? You likely have so many questions to ask on this topic and this guide is where you will get all the answers you need and more. Within these pages is information that will enlighten you, transform you and improve your life. In this guide, you'll get insight on Stoicism. Together, we'll take an in-depth look into its intricacies.

The nuggets contained in this guide will show you how Stoicism can help you to conserve time, improve your concentration skills and be more grateful for the good things that do come your way. Learning about Stoicism can help to improve even workplace dealings because, with it, you can see how to deal with any 'difficult' clients you may come across at work. For a school of thought that is hardly given a second thought by many people, Stoicism does present numerous benefits to those who practice it. This is a way of life that has helped countless people from ancient cultures to contemporary and is sure to be equally beneficial to you as well.

Dive into this guide and get to know the main ideas behind Stoicism. You'll discover various aspects of the practice, take a look at the lives of famous Stoics and learn Stoic exercises that can help you live each day happily and contentedly. The sooner you start reading, the sooner you can begin to enjoy a life of satisfaction and fulfillment.

Chapter One: Stoicism And Why You Should Be Interested

Ever heard the word "Stoic"? If you have, there is a fair chance it was used in a negative context. In our society today, many people associate the word Stoic with a complete indifference to all kinds of emotions. The general misconception is that Stoics are impassive people who aren't swayed by any emotion at all, be it love, pain, joy, or any other emotion. Stoicism is a school of philosophy that has been around since as far back as the 3rd Century BCE. At its core are values that are completely different from the common misconception. It makes use of personal ethics and methods to gain wisdom that are tailored and practicable for each person. When unfavorable events happen, Stoics believe that we don't actually react to them. Rather, they believe we act according to the way we view such events and that is completely in our hands.

From the Hellenistic period to the Roman era, Stoicism was one of the major schools of philosophy practiced. Its history is divided into three phases which are the Early Stoa, Middle Stoa and Late Stoa. Since its inception, it has been embraced by many notable people but the mastermind of this school of thought was Zeno of Citium, a Greek philosopher in Athens. The practice has evolved in many ways, but its basic teachings remain relevant, even to this day. Stoicism holds that humans acquire bad emotions when they make bad judgements. Therefore, Stoics reduce the chances of getting these bad emotions by exercising control over their mindsets and it works like a charm! They believe that when we take control of our emotions, we grow in harmony with our existence and in turn, become happier and more peaceful. It is believed that we can only achieve true happiness through four cardinal virtues which are Wisdom, Courage, Temperance, and Justice. Each of these virtues are subdivided into further virtues which all Stoics live by.

Stoicism is presented as a way of life through which its practitioners can transform into true embodiments of virtue and wisdom, known as Sages. A Sage is a person who has reached the peak of perfection morally and intellectually. Many Stoic philosophers shared the belief that genuine happiness is achieved by being virtuous and for that reason, a Sage wouldn't be swayed by any kind of misfortune. Lost a job? Lost a loved one? Stoic Sages see these as natural events that are simply out of our control. This is because that which we call misfortune causes us to be sad and through acts of virtue, there can be no sadness. When you start to see things from this perspective, you realize that you can gain even more control of your fate, so to speak. Keep in mind, however, that the early Stoics were not setting up a target for themselves to achieve. The practice wasn't started with the aim of being Sages. A Sage is a sort of ideal which all Stoics are encouraged to live up to and is not the primary objective of practicing. The point of Stoicism isn't for you to be able to add the title "Sage" before your first name after carrying out all the Stoic practices you've ever heard of, far from it. Rather, what really matters is setting yourself on the path to attaining Stoic Sage by improving yourself, by improving the ideas that go through your head and by improving the way you relate to and interact with people around you. Stoic philosophy is categorized into three main divisions: Ethics, Physics, and Logic. Each of these divisions plays a crucial part in helping us gain a deep understanding of Stoicism and how it can be applied to human life.

Unknown to many, Stoicism has had an unimaginable influence on general ethical thought from early Christianity to modern times. Morally, Stoicism's major goal is for its adherents to remain free from any sort of distress or suffering by seeking reason, actively and unemotionally. It urges people to remain objective in all situations so that we can make judgements that preserve our happiness. The Ethics division of Stoic philosophy is concerned with how we ought to live our lives. Stoics react passively to all external events because they believe that none of these events are good nor bad. Regardless of the highs or the lows that life brings with it, they maintain calmness knowing that allowing situations to alter their perception can be detrimental to their wellbeing.

By becoming disciplined and objective thinkers, it becomes much easier for us to really understand the natural universal reason behind all things. When people act mean or unkind to others, Stoicism helps us to understand that the person in question is simply ignorant of his or her own universal reason. From a Stoic standpoint, only ignorance can breed evil and unhappiness in an individual and this can only be corrected by practicing Stoic philosophy. When we take time to examine our thoughts and actions, we can then uncover the exact point where we might have deviated from our natural universal reason. Stoicism encourages us to live in line with our nature and this does not only apply to the laws of the universe but to our natural reason as well. To live in accordance with virtue and reason translates to becoming one with the universe, acknowledging that we all share one common reason and that each person, regardless of background and social standing, plays an important role in society.

Early Stoic philosophers viewed logic as anything that had even a tiny connection to rational thinking. With logic, it was possible for them to explore the other branches of philosophy as much as they needed to. Stoics likened this branch of philosophy to the shell of an egg in which other branches such as Ethics and Physics are contained. Ancient logic was a very broad segment and it touched on areas like grammar, epistemology, rhetoric, and so on. Western grammar as we know it today received many contributions from ancient Stoics. They helped to name the parts of speech we now refer to as Conjunctions, Articles, Adverbs and so on. Stoic rhetoric was like any other classical rhetoric we may recognize but the major difference was that it was very brief and straight to the point. Philosophers of that era were not people to spend time appealing to the emotions of their listeners while speaking. They merely said what had to be said in the clearest way possible. Stoics paid a great amount of attention to moral uprightness and they also paid a great amount of attention to the way they spoke. They maintained that our moral character and speech are intertwined; therefore, you cannot be good at rhetoric unless you are a good person as well. They put every aspect of their lives under scrutiny to ensure that the lives they lived were objective and well-rounded.

Stoicism teaches that we can live a good and meaningful life only when we reason about the world correctly. It also encourages people to live in accordance with their true nature by recognizing the fact that we are all social animals with the ability to reason. This is where its epistemology comes to play: in order to reason correctly, there has to be a theory of knowledge. Stoics view sense-perception as the basis of all knowledge and believe that we acquire it through our five senses.

Ancient Stoics embraced the philosophy of Stoic physics and they used this to break down the natural processes that take place in the universe. This aspect of Stoicism helped them to shed light on the cycle of the universe. Stoic physics can be described in terms of three main tenets: Monism, Materialism and Dynamism. Stoics view the universe not only as a pantheistic deity but also as a material substance. Stoicism identifies the universe with God and sees the universe as an active life-giving entity that contains all that it needs within it and can support itself as long as these individual parts all work together. All these parts have the ability to interact and harmonize with one another. This school of thought is completely materialistic and it holds that everything is corporeal, even ideas like justice and wisdom.

Stoicism proved to be very beneficial to early philosophers and it helped them to live satisfying lives. You might be wondering, however, if this practice relates to modern society in any way. Is Stoicism still relevant in today's era when we have progressed from marketplace announcements to instant news feeds and society has become even more complex? Can the practice still serve its intended purpose? Definitely! For one thing, Stoicism was born in a time when there were many crises and unfortunate events. It's not surprising that it took off as much as it did back then because by practicing it, people found the much-needed peace and security they desired. In this modern era, as well, unpleasant events are no strangers to us and there is no better way to adapt than by learning about a teaching that helped people in ancient times to live happily even in the face of disasters. Stoicism is designed to suit all kinds of societies and help all kinds of people. You can be sure that this timeless approach towards life can help you deal with problems that arise even in this century we live in.

Chapter Summary

- Stoic philosophy teaches that only objective and unbiased thinkers can fully understand their universal reason.
- Bad emotions beget bad judgements.
- By taking full control of our emotions, we can be happier and more peaceful.
- Reasoning actively and unemotionally rids us of suffering.

In the next chapter, you will learn about the origins of Stoicism. We'll take a look at the first proponents of Stoicism and how significant the practice was in 300 BCE when it all started.

Chapter Two: The Origins Of Stoicism

Let us take a quick trip down memory lane. It's sometime around 300 BCE and Greece is a budding Western civilization. Greece has fought many wars and has conquered many lands. The period had been fraught with endless wars, bloodshed and uncertainty. Things must have looked pretty gloomy for the people who lived then. Imagine living in an era when you could simply be enjoying a relaxing evening in your home and the next thing you know, the land is being besieged by enemy troops. Nobody knew what could happen next and predictably, many Greeks back then must have lived with their hearts in their mouth. Who wouldn't?

Diseases were rampant as well and they killed off people in the hundreds. Society today has come a long way in handling outbreaks of disease and medical emergencies. Now, we have all sorts of scanners, machines and clinical equipment which make such situations less scary and prolong life. Those who lived then, though, didn't have the luxury of modern medical innovations and so, we can only imagine how traumatic an unfavorable diagnosis must have been, especially at a time when people saw illness as some sort of divine punishment. People definitely were not truly happy and to most people at that time, it must have seemed that it wasn't even possible to be happy. In spite of all of this, Stoics still believed that happiness was achievable as long as one was virtuous. They believed that *Eudaimonia* could be found by having complete reliance on one's inner self and that such virtue is based on knowledge.

The practice started as a Hellenistic philosophy when its founder, Zeno of Citium started to teach people at the painted porch, otherwise known as the Stoa Poikile. In fact, the word Stoic originated from this term, Stoa Poikile. It was in this open market that the original Stoics would meet and discuss philosophy. Maybe a marketplace wasn't the best location to teach people but we should keep in mind that Zeno of Citium had been shipwrecked a while ago and practically lost everything. At the time when he started this school, he had no money to buy a building so early Stoics had to make do with what was available: the streets of Athens. It's quite interesting to see how something that began in such a noisy area grew to become a philosophical school with thousands of adherents. As more people started buying into the idea, its followers grew and later on, the practice spread to Rome.

The ancient practice of Stoicism is divided into three phases and each phase is marked by particular events. The Early Stoa took place in the 3rd Century BCE and some philosophers from that phase were Zeno of Citium, Diogenes, Cleanthes and Chrysippus. After this phase came the Middle Stoa between the 1st and 2nd Century BCE and it had philosophers like Posidonius and Cato the Younger. The Late Stoa of Ancient Stoicism took place during the 1st and 2nd Century CE when people like Marcus Aurelius,

Seneca the Younger and Epictetus were some of the school's prominent philosophers.

Greek Stoicism covers the first and second phases of the school, beginning from the school's founding to the time when cities like Rome overtook Athens and became the region's ruling body. Although most of the early exponents of Stoicism were from the Eastern Mediterranean, this school of philosophy flourished greatly in ancient Athens. Zeno was a student of Crates of Thebes who was an important Cynic. It isn't surprising, then, that Stoicism was based on some of the moral ideas proposed by Cynicism. The popular philosophical school back then was Epicurism which holds that humans live in a materialistic world and have an accidental nature that is subject to pain or pleasure. Zeno opposed this and subscribed more to the ideas behind Cynicism, which value simplicity and virtue. He was sure, however, to distinguish between Stoicism and Cynicism by replacing some harsh principles upheld by Cynicism with moderate and practical ones that could actually work for the real world. After Zeno of Citium came Cleanthes who was his pupil. Cleanthes added little to the school as he mostly followed the teachings that Zeno had provided. Stoicism received some vital contributions after the death of Zeno thanks to Chrysippus of Soli. He helped to ensure that Stoicism remained one of the strongest schools of philosophy by building further on the foundations that Zeno had laid. He further developed the three parts of philosophy and even came up with a system of logic.

Around 100 BCE, the center of Stoicism gradually began to move from Athens to other cities like Rome and Rhodos. While Zeno had been quite unbending in his beliefs, Panaetius was more flexible and made huge progress at simplifying Stoic physics. Unlike Stoics before him, he wasn't particularly interested in Stoic ideas about logic. Thus, the Stoic philosophy became more similar to Neoplatonism and because of this, it became even more accessible. It was also Panaetius who introduced this philosophy to Rome. The values which Stoics lived by and promoted proved to be very useful to the Roman society. How so? Such values included performing one's duties diligently without challenging the order of things.

The Roman Empire occupied many territories and societies and, understandably, they needed these resources to be properly managed. The Stoic philosophy posits that external events cannot be influenced but our attitudes towards them can be controlled. It also teaches the importance of diversity and holds that we're humans first even though our roles in life may differ. These Stoic teachings helped to ensure faithful duty on the part of the Romans and it was a perfect philosophy for them as they wanted an empire that was all-inclusive, as encouraged by Stoicism. The Stoic universal approach to morality was another aspect of the practice that drew many Roman intellectuals to it. Although it was purely based on reason and nature, it still aligned with the common moral codes. Stoicism was based on ideas that were relatively new but it didn't belittle or diminish the standards that were already in existence during that time in Rome. Rather, these ideas complemented the society's standards. Cicero, a popular Stoic, was of the opinion that pursuing justice is every human's primary duty. He criticized any illegal or immoral possession of wealth and power and openly argued against these. Cicero's writings and speeches helped to establish the Stoic philosophy as the most prominent in Rome.

Stoicism in the Middle Stoa was far more eclectic than it originally was and with time, the school became disunited and quite controversial. Stoic philosophy would, however, stand the test of time. Why? Because it worked. It was a method that provided needed results when practiced correctly so it could never truly be forgotten or simply replaced. It was during the Middle Stoa that Posidonius mirrored Panaetius' ideas and became close to Aristotle and Plato; in fact, some consider Panaetius to have been a Stoic and a Neoplatonist at the same time. In Rome, one of those who embraced Stoicism was Cato the Younger. He associated himself more with the original Stoic teachings of Zeno and Chrysippus rather than with the refined teachings that his predecessors now believed and promoted. Cato the Younger went on to become a role model for Stoics who practiced during that era as he was very vocal in opposing Julius Caesar whose rule he didn't approve of.

Between the 1st and 2nd Centuries CE when the Late Stoa took place, the interest of Stoic philosophers had shifted from Logic and Physics to Ethics. This period of Stoicism is the most popular one because it is the only period which provides us with original writings that have survived to this day. In one of Seneca the Younger's writings, he made use of daily events to discuss moral issues and people still read these works today. Epictetus was another Stoic author whose works were published by a student of his; these works were widely read and still remain relevant today. One of the most prominent Stoics of the Late Stoa was the Roman emperor Marcus Aurelius. His *Ta Eis Heauton,* or *Meditations,* was initially written as a personal journal but today it is likely the most widely-read and discussed Stoic writing. It continues to serve as an inspiration to people around the world because Marcus Aurelius highlighted many concepts like world citizenship and self-discipline, concepts that are still significant in our modern world. His writings have served as a means of personal growth and improvement for Stoics globally and many consider it to be the last major work of the Late Stoa.

From Zeno of Citium to Marcus Aurelius, Stoicism has evolved to become a way of living that is both timeless and beneficial. Stoic philosophy was able to inspire all kinds of people: businessmen, slaves, athletes, emperors, etc. Even though philosophers of the Middle Stoa were able to broaden the scope of Stoic philosophy, the basic tenets which were established by its founder have not changed. Its values remain the same and that is why the practice could be adopted into various kinds of societies that came afterwards, including the modern one we live in today.

Chapter Summary

- Stoicism began during the 3rd century BCE.
- The school of thought was founded by Zeno of Citium.
- Ancient Stoicism is categorized into the Early, Middle and Late Stoa.
- Stoicism was based on some ideas proposed by Cynicism.

In the following chapter, you'll learn about four cardinal virtues that are at the heart of Stoicism and how you can develop these virtues.

Chapter Three: Stoic Philosophy And Virtues

What are virtues? Take a look around you. How many people would you describe as *virtuous* today? In today's society, people are only out for themselves, treat others unfairly and only want to acquire as much wealth as they can. Many are materialistic and their happiness is dependent on their possessions. I don't think a lot of people are virtuous today and I imagine that you think that, too. Ancient Stoics had four major virtues which they used to guide their actions and live meaningful lives. They even believed that the only path to *Eudaimonia* - true flourishing or happiness - is by being virtuous. We were born to live virtuously and align ourselves with nature. When we do that, it's only natural that we'll feel genuine happiness. The four virtues that Stoics believe in are Wisdom, Courage, Justice and Temperance. Zeno of Citium made use of some of the teachings of Socrates, Aristotle and Plato to create a foundation for these four cardinal virtues. He saw these virtues as tools that are needed for man's highest good. This is because learning and honoring these virtues helped people to train their minds and act virtuously.

Stoicism teaches that the most vital thing for us as humans is to recognize that wisdom and virtue are the only things that are truly good and to live in accordance with them. Stoics believe that anything that is good is also morally perfect, therefore, a true Stoic would carry out an act that is virtuous simply because it is good to do so. Virtuousness would help you to avoid doing things that are morally imperfect and therefore evil. If the Stoics saw you as a virtuous person, then you were good. Being good ought to keep you happy. Let's take a look at each of these virtues and how you can start to develop them.

Wisdom

The virtue of Wisdom can be said to be the most essential of them all. Yes, all four virtues are vital but how do you determine when and how they should be applied? Through wisdom. With it, you can determine the kind of situations where they should be applied and just how much of it you need. Stoics see wisdom as the ability to differentiate between that which is good, bad or indifferent. Wisdom is essential: it is the knowledge and experience you need to guide you through the world smoothly. I'd say someone who is truly wise has everything and the Stoics thought so, too. Ancient Greeks regarded it as the virtue of rulers because it allowed them to listen to advice and then act wisely based on their assessment. Wisdom is a virtue that they greatly prized, even during Zeno's time. In fact, he had something to say regarding the structure of our faces in relation to this. He said each person has one mouth and two ears for a reason: to speak less and listen more. He also said that having two eyes implies that we should observe and read more than we speak. Being prudent or wise includes having good sense, good judgement and being objective. As important as it was back then, Wisdom still plays a huge role in our lives today. Maybe it's even more needed than it was back then. We live in a digital age and, on the plus side, this means that information is readily available to us but is it the right kind of information? There's so much to digest. We need to know how to sort between the useful and useless and pick out information that will benefit us and give us the wisdom to live good lives. The value of studying and being open-minded cannot be overemphasized. Epictetus, one of the early Stoics, said we cannot learn that which we think we already know. For this reason, it is of utmost importance that we remain humble students and keep seeking even more knowledge. We need to keep reading and learning with the goal of acquiring beneficial information. Filter out the background noise and focus on the key points which you need to absorb.

Wise people know how to grasp the truth about the things that truly matter and apply them accordingly to their daily lives. This is what Epictetus calls the Discipline of Assent. It deals with making right judgements about the events that take place in the external world and its nature. While incorrect judgements cause bad emotions, proper discernment builds excellent thoughts and actions. Proper judgement also helps us to enjoy good flow in our individual lives. The virtue of wisdom is linked with the ability to be completely honest with ourselves and with the people around us. Wisdom and self-deception cannot exist alongside each other and there can be no justice, either, as long as we're being deceitful.

There's so much insight available to us today and we can learn anything at all, right at our fingertips! Today, why not start to honor this vital virtue of wisdom? Learn to slow down, be deliberate and seek out the knowledge you need to transform your life.

Courage

Courage, sometimes called fortitude, is the ability to face danger, fear, difficulty, uncertainty, etc. This virtue was seen as a military virtue in Greece and it was a common trait amongst soldiers of that era. Courage determines our actions regardless of the way we feel. Contrary to popular opinion, courage is not the absence of fear; rather, it is being afraid and doing what is necessary, all the same. Ancient Greek soldiers were the models of heroism and courage. Not knowing what would happen during a fight, they'd still put on their armor and approach the battlefield, courageous and unflinching in the face of death. This doesn't mean that they never felt scared; they realized the need to remain strong. We can be said to be metaphorical soldiers: there are times in our lives when things just do not go the way we want and we're faced with many adversities. Be it a global pandemic or something less terrifying, sometimes living can become an act of courage. How can you deal with it?

Perspective is so important. Perspective can make all the difference between utter disappointment and simply taking unfavorable events as they come. The Stoics put this to good use. Rather than viewing tragedies or inconveniences as things that throw them off track, they learned to see them as opportunities and answers to questions they couldn't answer. For Seneca the Younger, it was people who had remained fortunate and had always had luck that were to be pitied. How do you learn when everything has been pleasantly rosy for you?

> "You have passed through life without an opponent. No one can ever know what you are capable of, not even you"
>
> **Seneca The Younger**

Trials are there to strengthen and mold us into the best versions of ourselves. Without trials, we cannot truly grow. Courage can also refer to being resilient. Courage can be found when you're holding on to your goals relentlessly even when faced with difficulties. Did you fail that test, even after taking it twice already? Do you have an opponent who is using shady methods to win that competition? Or maybe you picked a class in school and it's seeming much harder than you expected? There are endless examples that apply to this and I'm sure you can think of some, too. The virtue of courage involves perseverance, confidence and honesty at all times.

It is pretty easy, however, to mix up courage and stubbornness. There's a huge difference between the two, though, and the application of wisdom is the thin line that separates them. With each goal we chase, we need to ask ourselves the problems we're facing and why we're facing them. Most importantly, we need to question our intentions for each goal. It is impossible to act with courage if our intentions are vain or selfish. This is because such a goal has no virtue in it. It is necessary for each of us to remember to judge our actions wisely so that we do not get caught up and lose ourselves while pursuing virtue. Courage in the absence of wisdom becomes vanity and stubbornness. On the other hand, admitting your flaws and then putting in the effort to overcome them shows courage, self-reflection and is a behavior that is worthy of a Stoic.

To develop this virtue, you need to practice doing things that really scare you. Step out of your comfort zone and learn to push your limits. Apart from building your courage, this will also help to boost your confidence which seems to me like an awesome two-for-one deal. Confidence comes from knowing what you can handle and is a powerful tool when entering unfamiliar situations. It is worthy to note that doing things that scare you does not imply taking risks that are unhealthy and unnecessary. Taking a dive head-first into a waterfall or fighting a bear, for example, are not ways of showing courage. That's simply being unwise and risking your life. Doing things that you generally shy away from or give up on doing too early are great ways to begin.

Grab the microphone at the next conference and share your honest thoughts. Do some extra hours in the gym. Speak your mind. This way, you can be sure that you are becoming more courageous and improving your confidence as well.

With each adversity that comes your way, let your actions be guided by courage and let them help you to remember why this virtue is of huge importance. We can all be courageous. It's an ability that we're all born with and each day presents us with great opportunities to exercise that courage. It has been said that the decisions that scare us the most are the ones that will be most impactful in our lives. We need to try things that scare us on a daily basis so that we do not miss out on all the amazing blessings that life has to offer.

Justice

This is the bond uniting the three other virtues. Being just means being reasonable and fair especially with regards to decision making and the way other people are treated. All Stoic virtues are important but doing the right thing influences the others virtues and is therefore the most vital. The famous Stoic emperor Marcus Aurelius saw justice as the source of all other virtues. When you hear the word *justice*, you might be thinking of the legal sense of it like what is represented by courts, judges, etc. Stoics, however, see it as something much broader than that.

The Stoic virtue of justice is closely linked with the Stoic concept of *Sympatheia* which is the belief that everyone and everything in the universe is part of one big sacred whole. When we bear in mind that "all things are mutually woven together and therefore have an affinity for each other," we'll be prompted to be good people and also be good to others. We're all citizens of a single world and we all have the duty of looking out for and after one another. Imagine how the world would be if more people adhered to this. Maybe there'd be no homeless people on the streets; maybe there would be fewer wars; maybe we all would feel much safer in our environments than we presently do. Firm believers in nature and its beautiful designs, Stoics held that humans were naturally intended to be active helpers to one another. Although it might sound quite simple, it can be very easy to forget this. It's easy for us to think that we only need to worry about people in our immediate environment. We can easily get carried away with our own problems. To each his own, right? Not to Stoics. They believe that we were primarily designed to work together for the benefit of us all. Yes, it's common for people to fight or disagree but Stoicism holds that such acts are against our true human nature.

Ancient Greeks believed that a society can only be orderly through justice and just people create a just society. Throughout history, Stoics have been known to be great advocates of justice, even at times when it is dangerous for them to advocate this way. Armed with courage, another vital Stoic virtue, they do great things and go to extra lengths in the defence of the ideas and people that they love. To this very day, many politicians as well as activists have utilized the Stoic philosophy in strengthening themselves. Stoicism has helped to prepare them for the difficulty that comes with fighting for the right ideals and it has also served as a guide for them to discern between that which is right and wrong. Stoics have a deep belief in the ability of individuals and they believe that even one person can make a huge difference. No underrating is allowed in this school of thought. Everyone is capable of achieving great things and doing exploits. Being a successful politician or activist requires planning, realism, understanding and hope. Such an individual needs to be wise, accepting and be comfortable with saying "no" to the status quo. Apart from having a clear view of the world, Stoics also see what it is capable of being and to that end, they remain brave and act in strategic ways that help to transform that world into a reality.

Temperance

Being temperate means knowing that you have enough when you have just what you need. Oftentimes, Stoics interchanged temperance with self-control, which is the ability to control impulses and desires. We all know what it means to show self-control. The virtue of temperance, however, is even deeper than that. It involves exercising self-control even with things that are immaterial. It also deals with being fair and partaking in public service. Aristotle once referred to it as the *golden mean* because it is the virtue that lies in the middle. Temperance is the balance between dissatisfaction and discontent.

> "...because most of what we say and do is not essential. If you can eliminate it, you'll have more time, and more tranquility. Ask yourself at every moment, "Is this necessary?"
>
> Marcus Aurelius

Keeping this quote in mind in every situation will help us to live well-balanced lives without relying on temporal pleasures for our happiness. How much do you really need? How far do you really have to go? Are you focusing on essential things? Temperate people are forgiving, humble, orderly and always exercise self-control.

Remember when we talked about the virtue of Courage? As vital as it is, we also know that bravery can easily become recklessness when it puts the lives of the person in question in danger as well as those around them. This is where temperance comes in. Aristotle explained that there is cowardice, a lack of courage and there is recklessness which is an excess display of courage. Temperance is the guide that helps us to know just how much is too much. It involves doing good things and doing them in the right amount. When we allow ourselves to get carried away with the fleeting happiness that comes with having too much, we lose appreciation for the things that really matter and throw ourselves off track. This virtue helps us to be disciplined and organized in all areas of our lives. For instance, working to earn a living is great, but working so much that you have time for nothing else isn't being temperate. That way, you're missing out on other things that are also vital such as your relationships, recreation and relaxation. On the other hand, not working at all shows a lack of temperance. People who do not work can miss out on things that spice up our lives. Everybody needs income but having self-control will help us to realize that we always need to balance work and leisure when it can be so easy for us to fall from one extreme to the other. This virtue helps us to realize that in life, situations come and go but our reality is based on how we react to those situations. Starting today, bear this important virtue in mind. Stop allowing yourself to swing from one edge to the other. Try to be temperate in everything you do and you'll be more than glad you did.

In conclusion, these were the four virtues the Stoics thought were beneficial. Compared to these four virtues, nothing else was valuable. They had every reason to think so because there's no event or challenge that's so intimidating that these four virtues cannot solve. They're all important and we cannot neglect one and honor others if we truly want to live fulfilling lives. By learning the best ways to embody these virtues, we can be sure that we are on our paths to having prosperous lives. Sure, there could be times when you feel a little confused about the right action to take. When this happens, go for the ones that are in total alignment with a virtuous path. That way, you'll live happily and successfully. Remember to keep seeking knowledge and act wisely.

Chapter Summary

- Wisdom guides us on how to be in smooth existence with nature.
- Courage helps us to face the adversities life throws at us.
- Justice motivates us to be good people to ourselves and to our neighbours.
- Temperance helps us to find the right balance between two extremes.

In the next chapter, we'll take a look at some crucial Stoic principles and how we can apply them properly in our lives.

Chapter Four: Eight Vital Stoic Principles To Live By

Now that we have examined the four cardinal virtues of Stoicism, let's get practical. In what ways can we actually develop a Stoic mindset? We're not reading about these things just to know of them, we also need to put them into practice. One of the early Stoics, Epictetus, asked a vital question: "If you didn't learn these things in order to demonstrate them in practice, what did you learn them for?" It's not enough to simply be aware, taking necessary steps to cultivate them in daily life is most vital. Each one of us wants to live happily and reach the peak of our potential. That's exactly what Stoic philosophy is concerned about. Just think about the fact that you can be all you really want to be and be happy in the process. Discussed in this chapter are eight important Stoic principles that we can all tap into to help us live accomplished lives.

Always Seek Out Knowledge

Try to learn something new every day. Keep your mind open and be willing to discover new things. It isn't enough to learn only when the opportunity presents itself. We need to actively make time for it. Seneca the Younger was of the opinion that relaxation in the absence of learning is death and people who live this way are in figurative tombs. Modern society has access to more information more than it ever has before. It's unbelievably easy to learn something new because there are countless guides and videos to make learning fun for us. There's wisdom to be found in many places on the internet. There are cheap books containing valuable nuggets of wisdom that you can have delivered right to your doorstep. We can learn from some of the smartest people to ever walk the earth just by digging a little deeper. Learning is easier than we think and it is up to us to take the necessary steps to do so. Gaining wisdom will help us to be better people and to improve ourselves. It will also help us to be better friends, partners and parents to our fellow humans. On this subject, Epictetus likened education or learning to gold which is valued by everyone. There is really no excuse for you to defer your learning and, by extension, your growth.

Know The Difference Between Good, Bad And Indifferent Things

Early Stoics ensured that they put things in the categories they belong in. The *good* things are the four cardinal virtues while the *bad* ones are their opposites: cowardice, folly, indulgence and injustice. Indifferents include all other things but can identify as health, possessions and reputation. They are things that do not help us to flourish nor hinder us from doing so. Many people today would feel that these things can be good or bad but

Stoicism helps us to understand that they do not matter in reaching Eudaimonia.

Your general happiness is not determined by your riches or health status. These things are all indifferents as they simply don't matter. We need to cultivate the habit of neutrality regarding indifferent things and learn to be content with what nature throws our way. Although things that are indifferent cannot be good in the true sense, there are indifferents that are of greater value and higher preference than others. The Stoics were very logical in their interpretations and so they created a distinction between *preferred indifferents* and *dispreferred indifferents*.

Indifferents are things that aren't exactly good or bad. Preferred Indifferents are indifferents we'd rather have in comparison to other indifferents. For example, wealth is seen as an indifferent but at the same time, it's great to be able to afford things. The balance comes, however, from realizing that you do not need to have wealth before you can live a life that is virtuous. It's only natural to opt for good health instead of illness, happiness over sadness, riches over poverty and so on. We're allowed to seek these things but while doing so, we need to be sure that our integrity is not compromised and that we are living virtuously. This implies that we would see the need to endure sickness or poverty honorably rather than seeking preferred indifferents in a shameful manner. Having friends, too, is seen as a preferred indifferent for many but Stoics would always consider virtue before friendship. A Stoic would not lie to save a friend because they believe that friendship is of little significance compared to justice. According to the Stoic philosophy, it's what you do with your resources that count, that your actions or behaviors are the only things you truly have control over so make sure that they are in tune with the things that really matter.

Speak Only What Is Necessary

Have you ever been in a room with people who simply cannot stop talking about themselves? Every chance they get, they're always ready to make themselves the main topic of discussion and center of attraction. Regardless of the topic being discussed, there's a part of their lives that can be used as a conversation booster. Being with people like these can be tiring. We need to avoid talking about ourselves at every chance we get because that way we can miss vital information. When all we want to do is talk, we can't listen to understand because we're busy thinking of the next thing to say. Rather than complaining, gossiping or spending a great deal of time talking about mundane things, we should learn to listen to people and understand what they're trying to say. Talking too much is a turn-off for many people.

> "It is better to trip with the feet than with the tongue"
>
> **Zeno of Citium**

By keeping this essential admonition in mind, we'll see the need to speak when spoken to and to speak only what is necessary.

Learn To Ask Yourself What Could Go Wrong

A popular Boy Scout motto urges us all to *Be Prepared*. This motto reminds us to be ready for whatever life throws at us and we can all agree that this motto is relevant in many situations. Medically, vaccines are substances that prepare the body to fight off infections before actually accessing our bodies. After being vaccinated, our bodies are prepared to handle any health issues that may come up as a result of infections. Similarly, Stoics believed that every human being needed to develop the habit of 'preparing' their minds for 'misfortune.' In fact, one major reason why people study Stoicism is to know how to remain calm in the face of trouble. This is because Stoics have trained themselves to the point that they are free from emotional distress when they face situations that seem like hardships. They believe that what we see as misfortunes are actually indifferents which can be tackled rationally, patiently and calmly. Stoicism advises us to premeditate adversity so that we know the best ways to handle them if and when they do come. With each decision you make, ask yourself, "What could go wrong?" and know how to plan for any eventuality. This is not the same thing as dwelling on negativity. Instead, it is simply preparing yourself mentally and arming yourself with a backup plan that you can always fall back on. At the same time, it is worthy to note that this anticipation does not automatically mean that we'll become figurative 'rocks' who can't feel a thing no matter what is thrown at us. This preparation helps to cushion the effects of challenges and allows us to think rationally and make the wisest decisions we can.

> "Nothing happens to the wise man against his expectations"
>
> **Seneca the Younger**

This approach implies that a wise man is well-prepared at all times. There's nothing that can catch such a person off guard or throw him off track. While it would be completely absurd to hope we face difficulties in life, it would be equally absurd to think that our lives will be just peachy. Preparing our minds by imagining tough scenarios will help us to be stronger and invulnerable in real-life situations.

Search For The Opportunities In Difficult Situations

The act of discovering opportunities is the same idea as seeing the silver lining in every cloud or making lemonade when life pelts you with lemons. The Stoics believed in looking for opportunities for growth in every challenge that came their way. Regardless of the event, they would always pick the most virtuous choice between fighting through these challenges and cowering before them. It's the way we view things that matters since life's many challenges are only hindrances if we allow them to be. We can either see them as opportunities to learn and broaden our minds or barriers that will hinder us. It all rests with our perception. The way you interpret or react to a challenge will determine how successful you'll be at overcoming it. Any challenge we face can only have strength when we give it to them; at the end of the day, it's what you do with it that matters. This principle will be of immense benefit to us because it reminds us that we always have the choice of thriving despite a challenge or shrinking because of it.

Love Everything That Happens

Stoics strongly believe in the principle of *Amor Fati* which encourages us all to accept and love whatever happens. This is because we're only going to suffer if we start to deny the reality of things or think that things are working against us. Although it can be a tough pill to swallow, we need to acknowledge the fact that there's a higher force at work and that we do not have control over everything happening around us. In many instances, it's much easier to change our opinions about unfavorable events than it is to change the actual events. While the event is already in the past and cannot be changed, we still have our opinions. We need to learn to stop worrying about the things we could have instead of enjoying the things that we do have. Stoic philosophy refers to it as the "art of acquiescence" which means accepting what is instead of constant denial over everything. One way we can start to imbibe the principle of *Amor Fati* is by accepting that we have no control over events that happen and that anything that does happen is fine. Just like the weather, we're not in charge and that's a truth we need to accept. Another way is by enjoying each ugly situation that comes our way and realizing that they can be vital for our growth.

Spend Your Time Wisely

We all know that the time we have to live is finite and that we're mortals. It's easy to doubt if this is really so because so many of us are living contrary to that knowledge. It's so easy for us to keep accepting situations that don't bring us complete fulfillment. Life is only so long and the most valuable resource we have at our disposal is time. Starting from today, try to live your life to its maximum and your future self will be thankful to you. Realize that time really is money and learn how to be thrifty with it.

Be Kind To People

In today's society, many people see a display of kindness as a show of weakness. They believe that it is each man for himself and that they do not need to worry about anyone else. Stoics, however, see being able to show kindness as a unique opportunity. They believed that we have the power to make someone happy and we should do so at every chance we get: compliment people, say thank you, smile warmly at someone. Regardless of the character flaws that a person has, learn to love them wholeheartedly and remind yourself that these flaws are only there because they cannot distinguish good from evil. Marcus Aurelius saw kindness as an invincible trait because even the meanest person is rendered powerless if you keep being kind to them. That must have been where the advice of "killing them with kindness" originated from. The next time someone speaks rudely or acts horribly towards you, accept it for what it is and always react with kindness and tolerance. Learn how to show your strength by being kind at all times. That's the best you can do.

Ancient philosophers were not okay with just learning about things. They saw the need to practice and also train themselves rightly. This is because we can easily forget the things we have learned and end up doing the opposite of those learnings as time goes by. For that reason, it is vital that we do not allow ourselves to simply learn these Stoic principles and then forget them. It can be quite overwhelming to take on all of these principles at once.

Studying requires time, patience and full devotion. It'll be much easier for us to sit back, reflect and decide on one principle to begin with. So that's a task we all have to undertake: choose one of these eight vital principles and start imbibing them with effect from now. You'll thank yourself for it later on.

Chapter Summary

- Each day, set a goal to learn something new.
- There are good things, bad things and indifferents. Know the difference and learn to align your life with things that really matter.
- Show kindness towards people, even if they're unkind to you.
- Speak when necessary.
- Remember the principle of *Amor Fati*.
- See the silver lining in every cloud.
- Allocate your time wisely.
- Prepare your mind for worst case scenarios.

In the next chapter, we will take a look into the lives of famous Stoic philosophers and their thoughts on Stoicism.

Chapter Five: Famous Stoics And How They Lived

The Stoics of old were people just like us who came from all kinds of backgrounds. They were rich, poor, learned or not. They all shared a strong belief in the Stoic philosophy. Regardless of the circumstances they faced, they learnt to place their focus on only the things that mattered, the things within their control. They believed that it was their actions, thoughts and beliefs that made all the difference in living meaningful lives and this is why they scrutinized each action, thought and belief they had. These people were enlightened and curious individuals who saw the need to find answers to the numerous questions about our human nature and the universe. They placed huge importance on living virtuously and in true accordance with nature. They were men like Zeno of Citium, Marcus Aurelius, Epictetus, Seneca the Younger, Chrysippus to name a few. In this chapter, we'll shed some light on the lives of some major advocates of the Stoic philosophy that we are all familiar with today.

Zeno Of Citium

Zeno lived from 336 BCE to 265 BCE and was the founder of Stoicism. Out of all the Stoics, he is one person whose discovery of philosophy is very interesting to read about. Zeno was on a voyage when the ship he was on sank and took all its cargo with it. Rather than ending up in Piraeus, his initial destination, he landed in Athens which would later become the origin of Stoicism. It was while visiting a bookstore there that he became acquainted with Socratic philosophy and later on he met Crates who was an Athenian philosopher. These two occurrences changed his life unimaginably and eventually helped him to develop the principles behind Stoic philosophy.

Zeno began to teach his philosophy at the Stoa Poikile, a porch from which the name "Stoicism" was derived. We need to note, however, that Stoicism wasn't the original name of this philosophy. Zeno's followers were referred to as Zenonians before they were identified as Stoics. It was clear to Zeno that people suffered because they feared losing things that were dear to them or they suffered because they were constantly chasing things they didn't have. He proposed that humans need to rely on their reason instead of on pleasures as doing that would help us to realize that nothing lasts forever or remains valuable forever. He said that we need to achieve a state of Apatheia which would help to set us free from enslavement by our own passions. Sadly, none of Zeno's writings have survived to this day but we can find some quotes about him in certain philosophical books.

Stoicism has gone through many developments since it was first proposed but Zeno's initial message is still very much alive: we can experience happiness by living a life of virtue and monitoring our emotions. After Zeno's death, ancient Athenians paid homage to him with a bronze statue which is still standing tall to this day. Only someone who had contributed immensely to the overall growth of a society could be bestowed with such an honor.

Marcus Aurelius

Marcus Aurelius was born in Rome in 121 CE and served as the Roman emperor from 161 CE - 180 CE. He was seen as the last of the five good emperors and was highly respected by Romans. Born into a privileged and prominent family, he was dedicated to learning and was fluent in Greek and Latin. Aside from his intellectual interests, Marcus also showed deep interest in the study of Stoic philosophy. He saw it for what it was, a school of thought that encouraged people to exercise reason, self-control and a strong belief in fate. He was known by many to be a hard worker who was also very serious-minded.

Although Marcus was born into a politically prominent family, not many people would have predicted that he would become the ruler of the Roman empire one day. During his reign as emperor, things were not rosy at the outset for him but he kept going. He used the ideas behind Stoic philosophy to develop efficient strategies to cope with anger and other vices. Aurelius was very good at controlling his anger because he was one of the few people who realized that while anger is a fleeting emotion, the damage it leaves can be permanent. Stoics saw anger as temporal madness and it's not surprising to find that Marcus constantly focused on anger-management strategies throughout his book *Meditations*. In the book, he spoke highly of the traits to be displayed by true Stoics. He urged us to value our reasoning above all else and to limit our desires and passions. Marcus used this book to examine topics like change, death, the value of rational thinking as well as living in full accordance with nature and accepting it.

Seneca The Younger

Lucius Annaeus Seneca was a Roman philosopher who adopted many Stoic viewpoints and also argued for them. He was born in Cordoba in 4 BCE and lived until CE 65. Some of his works on Stoicism have been read widely and a popular one is his *Letters from a Stoic* which serves as a guide for young people just starting their Stoicism journey. Seneca's interest in Stoic philosophy was planted by one of his early teachers who was a Stoic and an admirer of Cato the Younger's teachings. Seneca admired Cato and even referred to him in many of his writings. He didn't, however, limit himself to only studying Stoicism and borrowed from other schools as well. In addition to writing about philosophy, Seneca also made sure to explain what he'd learn in practical ways that we're actually meant to use. His works are some of the most enjoyable Stoic works because they come in the form of letters which make them easy to read and grasp.

Conditions were not always favorable for Seneca and he had a deep personal knowledge of ways by which we could deal with the two extremes of fortune. His life was filled with many ups and downs. He went from being very rich to being exiled and eventually committed suicide at the order of Nero who was his pupil. Until his death, he bore it all gracefully. He obviously had to walk many difficult paths but he made sure that he lived with self-awareness and reflection as much as he could.

Epictetus

Epictetus was a Greek philosopher who was born around 50 CE and lived until 135 CE. He was born into a wealthy home as a slave in Hierapolis, now known as modern-day Pamukkale in Turkey. His owner gave him the chance to study liberal arts and it was during this time that he started learning about philosophy. Shortly after the death of the infamous emperor Nero, Epictetus gained his freedom and began to teach philosophy, a task he committed himself to for almost 25 years. He taught philosophy until emperor Domitian decided to banish all the philosophers in Rome around 93 CE. When that happened, Epictetus relocated to the Greek city of Nicopolis and created a philosophy school where he taught until he died. For Epictetus, we all have a choice to either chase material wealth, like many people do around us, or to walk the path of philosophers. In those days, philosophy was not just a subject: it was a way of life.

Philosophers made genuine efforts to master how to live successful lives. The Stoics believed that living by this philosophy was the best way to truly understand our minds. They believed that people who know how to control and harness their thoughts have a greater chance of reaching *Eudaimonia* than people who think that they need to meet some societal standards to be happy.

> "Some things are up to us and some are not up to us. Our opinions are up to us, and our impulses, desires, aversions- in short, whatever is our own doing. Our bodies are not up to us, nor are our possessions, our reputations, or our public offices…"
>
> **Epictetus**

This quote by Epictetus helps us to realize that attaching our happiness to things that are outside our control, things such as health, wealth etc., will only cause us much suffering. Epictetus encouraged us to be content in all circumstances and be happy with our reality. One interesting thing about Epictetus is that he never actually penned his teachings down. It is through one of his students that we have written versions of his lessons. One thing we do know is that all kinds of people found solace and wisdom in his Stoic teachings. No doubt, we can find many gems in these writings, as well.

Chrysippus

Chrysippus was yet another of the ancient Stoics whose lives we can use as beacons of light to guide us through life. He was born in Soli, now present-day Mersin in Turkey, in the year 280 BCE. Many people refer to him as the Second Founder of Stoic philosophy. Chrysippus was born into a wealthy family and inherited much property in his early years. He lost all these properties, however, when the ruling king confiscated them; he moved to Athens. It was in Athens that he received his first exposure to Stoicism and became a disciple at the Stoic school.

Chrysippus was known for being skilled at decoding and proposing many philosophical arguments and, shortly thereafter, everyone saw him as a confident and self-reliant person. Chrysippus was not comfortable with simply getting information from his teachers; he liked to use available information to come up with his own proof. After his former teacher, Cleanthes, ended his tenure, Chrysippus replaced him as the head of the school. The school constantly challenged his ideas as well as the broader aspects of Stoicism. He then decided to formalize some crucial Stoic teachings in order to protect the school of thought from possible attacks.

By combining the works of Zeno of Citium with Cleanthes, Chrysippus was able to organize vital teachings that served as foundations for Stoic philosophy. He was also able to create a detailed system of propositional logic which consists of if-then statements. We might be familiar with this form of logic now but at that time, it was a system that changed the way philosophy was studied. Like many other Stoics, Chrysippus believed that the events that occur in our lives are predetermined and are completely out of our hands. He was, however, a firm believer in personal freedom and the benefits of having individual knowledge of the world. He was an amazing writer and is said to have written a minimum of 500 lines on a daily basis, eventually writing more than 700 books during his lifetime, none of which have survived to this day. Some fragments of his writings have been discovered in other philosophical works but none of them is complete. Chrysippus was regarded as an expert in the fields of ethics, logic, physics and theory of knowledge. He died in the year 206 BCE from a supposed laughing fit during the 143rd Olympiad. The cause of his death has been widely debated for many years with some people blaming it on a short supply of oxygen and others on excessive drinking which resulted in a brief illness.

Cato The Younger

Marcus Porcius Cato or "Cato" for short is one of the names commonly associated with Stoic philosophy. He was born in Rome in 95 BCE and he remained an important figure throughout his lifetime. Cato was someone who stood firmly and forcefully against the dictatorship of Julius Caesar, even to the point of death. Many ancient Romans of that era had deep respect for him because he stood out as a symbol of morality, humility, integrity and dedication. Unlike countless Roman statesmen at that time, he remained incorruptible and never engaged in the corruption and bribery that was rampant amongst high-ranking officials. During his lifetime, Cato served as a senator and a soldier and was always in the public eye. This was majorly because of his role as the flag-bearer of the Roman Optimates, a group of traditionalists who greatly believed in the ancient rules that had preserved Rome. Cato was eloquent and a man of good character. He could always stand against Julius Caesar, his greatest enemy in both bravery and wit. He was someone who attained great heights in Rome's political space but he never wrote epics or letters to celebrate his numerous achievements nor did he pen down accounts of his military exploits. Cato's name was linked with many accomplishments but his intention was never to have it engraved on monuments. In fact, he didn't leave behind any essays or an autobiography of any sort. He was a staunch believer in the tenets of Stoic philosophy but he practiced it, as well. Cato preferred to live the ideal Stoic life rather than simply writing about it and he continued this practice to his dying day. He enjoyed living frugally and believed in leading by example. Even though Cato was well-to-do and could afford many luxuries, he chose to dress simply and even walked around barefoot. Cato's name has gradually faded in our society but one aspect of his life we can learn from and hold on to is his determination to live a life of virtue. He died in 46 BCE when Julius Caesar eventually ascended the Roman throne.

There were countless other people who subscribed to this school. Each of these people is exemplary and worthy of mention but cannot be discussed for lack of time. One thing, however, is certain: they all believed that virtue is the primary ingredient for happiness and they lived in alignment with this belief. They saw Stoicism as a way of life and honored its principles as much as possible. Can we take a cue from them? Can we live virtuously and train our reasoning, too? When we allow ourselves to listen and perform these principles like all these ancient philosophers did, our lives will surely be filled with joy, meaning and fulfillment.

Chapter Summary

- Zeno of Citium was the founder of Stoic philosophy and lived from 336 BCE to 265 BCE.
- Marcus Aurelius was a Stoic Roman emperor who lived from 121 CE to 180 CE.
- Seneca the Younger lived from 4 BCE to 65 CE and his works in the form of letters have survived to this day.
- Epictetus was born a slave around 50 CE and died in 135 CE.
- Chrysippus is referred to as the Second Founder of Stoic philosophy and he lived from 280 BCE to 206 BCE.

- Cato the Younger was born in 95 BCE and was a very vocal opponent of Julius Caesar. He died in the year 46 BCE.

In the next chapter, we will learn about the ways in which Stoicism has evolved and how it is being practiced in the 21st Century.

Chapter Six: Stoicism In Modern Times

The world has changed greatly from the first time Stoicism was proposed in Greece. Now, we worry about factors like climate change, social media, an overload of information. People who lived in ancient times had to deal with famine, slavery, war. These and other issues have been reduced as society has developed. There's no doubt that things have changed but reflecting on the ideas of Stoic philosophy will help to refresh our minds and understand its significance in our modern world. Although we may not have the exact challenges as the original Stoics did, one constant is the way we process challenges which is a major aspect of Stoicism. Unforeseen circumstances overtake us all, even to this day. Stoicism was an attempt by ancient philosophers to create solid tools to help us to process difficulties and also respond better to problems. And they did a pretty good job, didn't they?

How is this school of thought being practiced in the 21st Century? How has it evolved over time? Why are people as interested in it today as they were back then? Is it still relevant today? How so? These questions and more will be answered in this chapter.

Ancient Stoic philosophy can be described as a collection of opinions on Ethics, Physics and Logic. Stoic physics was concerned with the workings of the universe. Stoic logic dealt with making sound arguments. Stoic ethics focused on how to live a good and meaningful life. We should note that, even back then, there were already philosophies that focused on these areas as well. Ancient Stoicism was quite dynamic and as soon as more people started to embrace the practice, different interpretations began to emerge, too. The more the school's audience grew, the more Stoic philosophy began to undergo changes. Even though Stoic tenets are universal, there's no doubt that Zeno of Citium developed his teachings based on the culture and what was happening around him. When Stoicism moved from Greece to Rome, there was a change in the areas that the philosophy emphasized on because the Romans were more concerned than the Greeks were about how to achieve and retain order. The philosophy had to be tailored to fit the reality of the people practicing it.

Similarly, Stoicism has been influenced by the modern world and it has propagated and refined several strategies that are in tune with our present reality. Today, Stoicism has discarded the ancient Latin or Greek languages which ancient Stoic works were written in. This way, we can now get an even better grasp of the key concepts that are promoted by this philosophical school. While ancient Stoics had to gather round in person in one place to learn and argue about crucial matters, technology has made it much easier for us to access Stoic teachings through the internet and different social media platforms. Today, many people pay more attention to the works of Marcus Aurelius, Seneca and

Epictetus because they focus mainly on the aspects of Stoic philosophy that relate to our way of living. In the modern world, Stoicism is constantly being refined to ensure that contemporary areas of interest are also accounted for.

In recent times, there is a renewed interest in Stoic philosophy by people around the globe. It seems more people are starting to turn to this ancient wisdom for guidance, knowledge and enlightenment. One reason for this is how universal Stoic teachings are: they can work for every and any one, regardless of background or location. At its core, Stoicism is concerned with managing our human nature as well as showing us how to enjoy the uncertainties of life. Human nature will always be universal as will the goal of living happily and therefore the advice that Stoicism gives us is applicable to everyone. The availability of information in the modern world is another reason why people are buying into the Stoic philosophy. We all know that there is an information overload in our society today. Everyone has something to say and, oftentimes, what is said is based on feelings and not facts. With Stoicism, we can all learn how to take better control of our lives and be more self-aware so that we do not simply get lost in the sea of information out there. Many years ago, various social institutions such as schools, family units and religious houses were where people could find meaning behind their existence. Most of these institutions are no longer as relevant in our present society and this lack of relevance has left many of us confused and hungry for counsel. More people are now finding solace in Stoicism which advises them on how to find some meaning in this wild world we live in. With Stoicism, we can all uncover practical steps to living productively and in harmony with the world.

To answer whether Stoic philosophy is still relevant in our modern society, let's ask ourselves two important questions: First, is life still full of ups and downs? Second, do we still experience difficulties today? Of course, the answer to both questions is yes. Like in the time of the Greek and Roman philosophers, life sometimes places us in unwanted situations. We might not get what we want all the time; people might treat us wrongly; the list is endless of the ways we can be mistreated or be faced with difficulties. The nature of problems people faced then compared to what is faced now might have changed in one way or another but, still, we all face problems. The wisdom found in Stoicism is timeless and its philosophy provides us with answers to pressing questions about life that many people don't even consider asking. So many subjects are taught in modern classrooms but nobody ever really talks about the proper way to live and find meaning. Stoic philosophy is practical and shows us how to handle both good and bad events successfully. It also provides us with exercises that teach us how to live virtuously and remain focused. Stoicism is appropriate for anyone who is faced by uncertainty. It's teachings can, therefore, be said to still be relevant today.

Practicing Stoicism isn't a one-day affair. It requires our constant effort to tap into its immense blessings. When we cultivate Stoic qualities, even in times that favor us, we will learn how to act in line with them when we seem to be in dire need of them. It can be likened to going to the gym: you might not like or even understand the reason behind it at first but, with dedication, you'll begin to see its benefits. With time, it'll become second nature for you. Instead of dreading it, you actually begin to feel excited about it. Similarly, the more you practice and seek knowledge about Stoic philosophy, the more enlightened you'll become. With time, it'll become a way of life for you and you'll find the peace and tranquility that comes with guarding your emotions and not allowing factors out of your control to affect your happiness. Rather than attempting to control the events happening around us, we need to be sure that we have full control over our own emotions. This is because our supposed control over these events is influenced by many external factors but the control of our own feelings is the only kind that can actually work out for us.

Chapter Summary

- Reflecting on Stoic philosophy helps us to realize its place and value in our lives.
- Stoicism is becoming increasingly popular because it is an appropriate philosophy for the modern world.

- Rather than trying to exert influence over external events, we need to train ourselves to not be misguided by our emotions.
- Stoic teachings have evolved overtime and are more in tune with our current reality.

In the next chapter you will learn the benefits of Stoicism and how embracing the practice can improve your life.

Chapter Seven: How Stoicism Can Help You

We have discussed many areas of the Stoic philosophy but we have not really highlighted the ways it can benefit you. As we have mentioned in this book, the only thing you have full control of is the way you perceive or view things. When you understand this, you'll see the need to think things through adequately instead of reacting with sentiment. Even more people are coming aboard the Stoicism ship today and they're already seeing how much of a valuable tool it can be. They're discovering the several ways it can help them to gain clarity, reduce their anxiety and even help them to make the best use of their resources. Stoicism can help you in these ways and more, including those listed below.

Remember What You Can Control

We all have our hopes and aspirations. We also have things that scare and frustrate us. Life can be tough, sometimes, and if we allow ourselves to, we'll focus more on the things that frustrate us rather than the aspects that motivate us to keep going. With Stoicism, we learn to understand that those things are simply indifferents that are neither good nor bad and it is our reaction to them that determines how we see them. We tend to spend precious time worrying about the things we can't control instead of giving that energy to the things that we actually can.

Feel More Fulfilled

Naturally, humans tend to engage in unnecessary comparisons. We envy people who we feel are happier than we are or have luxuries that we desire. While we're busy comparing our lives with the lives of other people we envy, it can be so easy for us to forget that we have all we need to be strong and happy. Ancient Stoicism urges us to practice poverty so that we can see that it isn't something to fear. Doing this helps us to realize the futility in feeling bad about what we don't have when we already have all that we need to live happily.

Conserve Your Time

It can be quite overwhelming to see people around us die. It has a weird way of reminding us that we are mortals who have a finite period of time to live. Is this a depressing thought for you? While it can be for some, this was knowledge that was rather motivating for the Stoics. It helped them to see the urgency in living purposefully. Seneca urged us to prepare our minds as if we have come to the end of life. By living each day as if it were your last, you can be sure that you'll make better use of your time. You'll feel even more alive and aware on a daily basis when you bear in mind that it may be the last time you're doing it.

Eliminate Anxiety

There are more people living with anxiety today than ever before. Many people feel conflicted about whether they're doing what really matters and they feel scared about what the future holds. Stoic teachings show us how we can take action on the things that are within our control and forget about other factors. Forgetting about other factors is definitely not as easy as it sounds but you'd agree that fearing the future while you can act on the present is quite pointless. The only time we have to make changes that will affect our future positively is now. Many of us do not bother to separate the things within our control from the ones we have no control over and that is why we worry about insignificant things. Stoicism helps us to identify these issues that are or aren't under our control thereby making it possible for us to enjoy peace of mind and tranquility.

Be Less Concerned About The Opinions Of Other People

Many people say that they do not care about what people think of them. Most times, this isn't quite true. It can be very difficult for us to ignore the opinions of people who we care about and who care about us, too. It can also be quite taxing to live our lives based on our own judgement but this is exactly what caring less about people's opinions entails. It's easier to simply do what we're told to do so that if things go wrong, we have someone to blame but that isn't a really fulfilling way to live, is it? Everywhere we go, people will have varying comments to make about us, our looks or our decisions. Although they might mean well, we cannot listen to all of them. Practicing Stoicism helps to improve our discernment abilities so that we entertain opinions that match with our ideals, and not just because we like what they have to say.

Boost Your Concentration Skills

Nowadays, there's entertainment everywhere we turn, as though people are constantly begging to be heard. There are countless shows for us to watch on TV, endless podcasts on every topic imaginable, business adverts, the list goes on. It's an entertainment whirlpool out there and if we allow ourselves to, we'll get sucked in. The more we allow ourselves to consume, the more we thirst for even more. Many people turn to different means of entertainment to keep themselves from getting bored or feeling alone with their thoughts. This kind of coping mechanism makes it hard for us to be the best versions of ourselves. At first, these mediums can be ways to keep boredom at bay but as time goes on, they could easily become means of distracting ourselves from our emotions rather than learning from them. If your first instinct is to turn on the TV when you feel sad or angry, then you cannot learn from these emotions and get rid of them. Stoic philosophy helps us to see the need to scrutinize our emotions and know how to make better decisions when you experience them, rather than looking for ways to avoid them.

Cultivate Good Spending Habits

How are you spending your money? True, no one can tell you how you should spend money you earned but are you spending wisely? Do you plan your expenditure or do you just dole out cash as you please? Are you an impulsive buyer? The Stoic philosophy helps us to see money as a resource that we need to put to good use. It also shows us the need to properly track our spending so that we ensure we're spending to produce great results instead of wasting it.

Be More Grateful

Stoicism helps us to view setbacks or challenges as an opportunity for improvement. Many of us spend too much time worrying about the what-ifs and not enough time appreciating things that are actually there. When we learn how to handle the challenges that come our way, we'll know how to appreciate the good times even better. We'll also feel more peace and contentment when we see such challenges as opportunities for growth that we need to cherish.

Chapter Summary

- Stoicism helps us to keep track of the things within our control.
- We care less about people's opinions when we practice Stoicism.
- Stoicism helps us to live satisfying lives.
- By ridding us of anxiety, Stoicism helps us to enjoy tranquility.
- We appreciate the good times better when we practice Stoicism.
- Stoicism boosts our concentration levels.
- Practicing Stoicism reminds us of the urgency in living purposefully.
- Stoicism shows us the need to spend our time wisely.

In the next chapter you will learn 20 valuable Stoic practices that will help you on your journey to becoming a Stoic.

Chapter Eight: Twenty Stoic Exercises To Explore

Practicing Stoic philosophy in a practical way is even more important than learning about it. Here are 20 great exercises that you can use to begin your Stoic journey.

Imagine That Everything You Own Is Borrowed

Bear in mind that everything you think you own apart from your mind is not truly yours and can be gone suddenly. While you should enjoy them while they last, avoid getting too attached to them. The next time you say goodbye to your loved ones, imagine it as the last time you'll get to do so. Be aware of the temporariness of everything that is dear to you.

Think Of The Worst That Could Happen

Nobody wants the worst to happen but if it does happen, we need to be prepared. Visualize the things that could go wrong in your plans for the next few days and then work out a suitable response for them.

Other-ize

It's easier for us to maintain equanimity and be objective when other people experience difficulties. Therefore, think about unfavorable events that happen to you as though they happened to someone else.

Speak Less And Listen More

Gossiping about people and judging them are not very virtuous things to do. We should only speak when necessary and, when we do, we should only speak about things that are actually beneficial. Pay attention to your conversations and make a conscious effort to be supportive and listen to people.

Apply Reason And Virtue Constantly

Regardless of the event or challenge, there is always an avenue for us to display virtuousness. Each time you find yourself in a tricky situation, ask yourself how you can show virtue and reason.

Make Use Of The Reserve Clause

We only have control over our thoughts and ideas. Therefore, when you plan to do something with an unpredictable outcome, make use of reserve clauses such as "fate permitting" and so on. This helps you to feel at peace and be more accepting of whatever outcome you get.

Choose A Role Model

For the Stoics, the Stoic Sage was a model of what they were aspiring to. Having such a role model helped them to be more aware of their actions. Imagine that your own role model is observing you and ask yourself what the person would do in everyday situations that you face.

Test Your Limits

When we have everything we need, we tend to undervalue these items and take them for granted. You'll appreciate these things even better when you stay away from them for a while. Restrain yourself from purchasing such things such as new clothes, morning coffee and so on for a few days and then relish them properly the next time you partake in them.

Reason First, React Later

Reacting emotionally to things outside our control is pointless as it is only our reaction that we have control over. Be mindful of how you react to your first impressions about people or things. There are occasions where you might not even need to react.

View Discomfort And Sickness As Opportunities To Be Virtuous

Any pain we feel is to the body and not the mind. We can choose to bear this bravely or to complain about it which doesn't do much at the end of the day. The next time you feel pain or fall sick, see it as an opportunity to develop your virtues and train yourself.

Forgive Easily

We all try to do what we think is right, even when it isn't. When people wrong us, they're merely acting out of ignorance and they deserve pity, not blame. Before you lose your cool over something, remind yourself that the person in question didn't know any better and so deserves your forgiveness and kindness.

Embrace Your Fate

It is better to accept and love your reality instead of wishing for it to be different. We cannot change the things that happen to us in life so it's better to accept fate as it comes instead of fighting it. When something happens to you and you have no power over it, ask yourself if you do have any power over it and if you do not, accept it however it is.

Imagine Your Life Has Ended

Doing this helps you to focus on the things that are essential and put your time to good use. Imagine that you died and you now have a second chance to live. Make two lists: one list of the things that matter to you the most and another list that shows what you actually do with your time. Compare both lists and pick out an area you can improve on.

Train Yourself For Uncomfortable Situations

This involves getting yourself uncomfortable so as to expand your comfort zone. This will help you to be more prepared for inconvenient situations. Put yourself in an uncomfortable situation from time to time: try sleeping on the floor for a night or going a week without your coffee.

Be Thankful For What You Have

It is better to value what you have instead of longing for what you do not have. Be thankful for the things you have and think of how much you'd want them if you didn't have them.

Remain Calm

Calmness even in the face of uncertainty was a primary goal that the Stoics sought to achieve. Make an active decision to not be bothered by unfavorable events that occur. Be more self-aware and tell yourself, "I buy tranquility instead," when someone or something tries to trigger or upset you.

Remind Yourself That Things Are Temporary

Nothing really belongs to us other than our minds. Things go missing; people pass on. Bear in mind that the people you love and life itself are precious because they may be gone suddenly. Take some time to think about your mortality and remember to always make the best of the limited time you have.

Do Some Daily Reflection

The most effective way to reflect yourself to yourself is to journal or write things down. Doing this helps you to go over the good things you did and motivate you to do more good things. Each night, take some time to ask yourself the good things you did during the day, ways you can do better, and how you can be the best version of yourself. Write them down.

Take The View From Above

Sometimes, we place our focus on things that are not as important as they seem to be. Taking the view from above helps us to view our problems with indifference and to realize that everything is temporary. Imagine yourself leaving your body and rising higher and higher into the sky while looking down on yourself and things that are around you.

Choose The Right Company

The friends you keep will have a huge influence on your way of living as well. If the people closest to you lack the right values, you eventually will lack them, too. Pay attention to the things you do and the people you spend your time with.

In the next chapter you will learn some Stoic techniques that you can make use of to get the best out of today.

Chapter Nine: Transform Your Life With These Five Stoic Techniques

To attain a life of virtue, we need to keep working to become the best versions of ourselves. By becoming who we really want to be, we're also finding our path to happiness. The first thing we need to do is to take control of our lives and who we are. It is by doing this that we'll discover our true selves and live with happiness and satisfaction. These techniques have been in use for several years and they are still relevant because they actually produce results. They are practical methods rooted in wisdom and common experience that will help to transform us into happier and better people.

Focus On Things Within Your Control

We cannot control the world and the things that happen in it but we can control our response to events through our reactions and judgements. It is inevitable that life will throw us into situations we can't control but it is the way we perceive and react to these situations that make them either good or bad. It is very important for us to know how to distinguish between the two and then choose our reactions appropriately. Apart from knowing how to differentiate one from the other, we also need to actively remember the differences between them. The more we do, the easier it will be to channel our efforts into becoming our best selves.

Curb Your Desires

One very important aspect of Stoicism is knowing how to train your desires. Most people believe that happiness comes from acquiring more and more things and they think all their problems will disappear when they have all they want. Human desires are insatiable and tying our happiness to the things we possess will only make us slaves to our desires. We'll only remain sad and disappointed if we keep chasing different things in a bid to feel fulfillment. It's okay to want things but we need to ensure they are things that really matter and to show appreciation for them.

Be Charitable

Contrary to popular opinion, you don't need to have a ton of money to be philanthropic. Even the poorest person can be a philanthropist: all it needs is a right attitude towards other people. We should try to bring everyone into a close circle and see them as fellow citizens of the world whom we have a duty to support. This helps us to not become excessively attached to a single individual and it's also a great way of expanding our cultural knowledge.

Live Simply

Stoicism shows us the need to simplify our lives and live with only the essentials. It shows us that the primary ingredient for a good life is our character. We have all we need to find true happiness. While there may be basic necessities, a lot of us have cluttered our lives with things that are neither necessary nor valuable. Although ridding ourselves of certain material things can be refreshing, we also need to get rid of any thoughts or actions that can prevent us from improving our lives. Scrutinize everything in your life and rid yourself of things that are not necessary.

Look Inwards

If you've been longing for freedom or peace of mind, one technique you can make use of is looking inside your own mind. It doesn't require more than 10 minutes. You simply need to block out the external world and practice looking inwards as your mind is the only place you can be truly free. When the external world seems chaotic, always remember that you can always find solace and comfort in your own mind.

With these techniques, we see how we can take a critical look into the way we live and make needed adjustments.

Chapter Summary

- Our views and reactions to life's events are what make them good or bad, not the events themselves.
- Human wants are endless. Attaching our happiness to our possessions will leave us sad and disappointed.
- All you need is the right kind of attitude to be philanthropic.
- Simplify your life by getting rid of unnecessary things and thoughts.
- Seek peace in your own mind when you need a break from the outside world.

In the next chapter, you'll learn some famous Stoic quotes and see how they apply to our lives today.

Chapter Ten: Famous Stoic Quotes You Can Use Today

It's like there's a Stoic quote for practically all situations. Feeling down? Sick? Lost a loved one? Need to calm your mind? Regardless of what we face, we can be sure that many ancient Stoic philosophers had to face similar battles. Experience really is the best teacher and these quotes were penned to serve as a motivation and a reminder that even though troubles may come, only people who make the best use of such situations and see them as learning opportunities will come out victorious. Below are some ageless Stoic quotes which can help you to boost your courage, calm your mind and bravely face whatever life throws at you.

> "Let us meet with bravery whatever may befall us. Let us never feel a shudder at the thought of being wounded or of being made a prisoner, or of poverty or persecution."
>
> **Seneca the Younger**

> "Curb your desire—don't set your heart on so many things and you will get what you need."
>
> **Epictetus**

> "Floods will rob us of one thing, fire of another. These are conditions of our existence which we cannot change. What we can do is adopt a noble spirit, such a spirit as befits a good person, so that we may bear up bravely under all that fortune sends us and bring our wills into tune with nature's."
>
> **Seneca the Younger**

> "I begin to speak only when I'm certain what I'll say isn't better left unsaid."
>
> **Cato the Younger**

> "To be even minded is the greatest virtue."
>
> **Heraclitus**

> "It is not the man who has too little that is poor, but the one who hankers after more."
>
> **Seneca the Younger**

> "The happiness of your life depends upon the quality of your thoughts."
>
> **Marcus Aurelius**

> "Fate leads the willing, and drags along the reluctant."
>
> **Seneca the Younger**

> "I love to go and see all the things I am happy without."
>
> **Socrates**

> "If it is not right, do not do it, if it is not true, do not say it."
> **Marcus Aurelius**

These Stoic quotes show how we can go through life's many challenges and still emerge happy and more self-aware. In modern lingo, it's called "glowing through what you go through." Use these quotes and sayings to reflect on the external world and use the knowledge from them to improve your life.

Conclusion

Stoicism is a philosophy that encourages us to review ourselves and the way we live in order to become better people. There are numerous other schools of thought that we can use to improve ourselves and live happily. Stoicism is a school of philosophy that is very practical and acknowledges our struggles. It doesn't shy away from the fact that life can be hard and that adversities are an inevitable part of life. Rather than running from our problems, Stoicism shows us how we can learn to accept our reality, be content with it and even better, make the best out of it. Stoic philosophy teaches us to seek happiness whilst improving ourselves and being the best we can be. This is the way that we can live maximally.

The information in this guide has been put together to make it easier for you to embrace Stoicism and understand its teachings. Cultivate the habit of accepting your reality and making the most out of it. This is the only way that you can truly flourish.

www.ingramcontent.com/pod-product-compliance
Lightning Source LLC
LaVergne TN
LVHW011739060526
838200LV00051B/3240